The Gospel of God,
One Word At A Time

Damaris Perry

WestBow
PRESS
A DIVISION OF THOMAS NELSON

WestBow Press books may be ordered through booksellers or by contacting:

WestBow Press
A Division of Thomas Nelson
1663 Liberty Drive
Bloomington, IN 47403
www.westbowpress.com
1-(866) 928-1240

Because of the dynamic nature of the Internet, any web addresses or
links contained in this book may have changed since publication and
may no longer be valid. The views expressed in this work are solely those
of the author and do not necessarily reflect the views of the publisher,
and the publisher hereby disclaims any responsibility for them.

ISBN: 978-1-4497-8459-1(sc)

Library of Congress Control Number: 2013902371

Printed in the United States of America

WestBow Press rev. date: 2/18/2013

As a young minister, many times I was approached and asked questions on various topics. People wanted spiritual guidance in certain areas. Thus, I received inspiration to write this book. I asked myself the question, "How can I give answers to simple issues that others deal with on a daily basis"? The Holy Spirit placed this book in my spirit to be a help to his children. They can learn what was in the mind of God when he created each of these words for mankind.

My focus in this book is primarily on the word of God and his thoughts concerning each word. The concept of this book will be addressed in three volumes, twenty-seven words in each volume. Three volumes, the three represents, the Father, Son and Holy Spirit. Twenty seven words in each volume. The two represents the relationship between the Father and Humankind. The seven represents the number of completion in the body of Christ. This book can be used as a guide to help people in their walk with God.

My prayer is that everyone that reads this book will be blessed, and find help and guidance in their day to day walk with God. I also pray that a fire be ignited or strengthened in each believer.

I love you. May God forever bless you.

BLESS:

The Lord has blessed us with His Word. All we have to do is be hearers, believers and doers of the Word.

Numbers 6:24-27 - The Lord bless thee, and keep thee: The Lord make his face to shine upon thee, and be gracious unto thee: The Lord lift up his countenance upon thee, and give thee peace. And they shall put my name upon the children of Israel; and I will bless them.

Psalm 103:1 - Bless the Lord, O my soul: and all that is within me, bless his holy name.

Acts 20:35-I have shown you all things, how that so laboring

ye ought to support the weak, and to remember the words of the Lord Jesus, how he said,

It is more blessed to give than to receive.

Points to Consider:

Numbers 6:24-27 - As people of God the Lord loves to bless us. He blesses us in a number of ways:

a. Shines his face: He gives us favor.

b. Gracious: No matter what we do , he always gives us a second chance.

c. Peace: God's peace is the peace that passes the test of time.

Psalm 103:1 - We must learn how to bless the Lord. We do-so with our heart (O my soul) and by having an open heart to do the right thing (saying no to ourselves and asking ourselves what would Jesus do?)

All that is within me: We should always look for ways to bless God in our everyday walk with him.

Acts 20:35 — As the body of Christ, the strong should always look for ways to help the weak. He said that it is always more blessed to give than to receive. Always look for ways to give your brother or sister a hands up.

Conclusion:

The Lord is showing us that blessings are more about us and we should bless the Lord with all our hearts. We should always look for ways to be a blessing by giving others a hand up, then the Lord will give us a blessing in shining his love, grace and his everlasting peace upon us.

Notes:

Blood:

The Lord has blessed us with His Word. All we have to do is be hearers, believers and doers of the Word.

John 6:53-56 - Then Jesus said unto them, Verily, verily, I say unto you, Except ye eat the flesh of the son of man, and drink his blood, ye have no life in you. Whoso eateth my flesh, and drinketh my blood, hath eternal life; and I will raise him up at the last day. For my flesh is meat indeed, and my blood is drink indeed. He that eateth my flesh, and drinketh my blood, dwelleth in me, and I in him.

Matthew 26:27-28 - And he took the cup, and gave thanks, and gave it to them, saying, Drink ye all of it; for this is my blood of the new testament, which is shed for many for the remission of sins.

Mark 14:23-24 - And he took the cup, and when he had given thanks, he gave it to them: and they all drank it. And he said unto them, this is my blood of the new testament, which is shed for many.

Points to Consider:

John 6:53-56 - The only way for us to truly dwell in him is to eat his flesh and drink his blood. We do that by becoming a part of the body. We have to dwell in the body for the body to dwell in us.

Matthew 26:27-28 - God paid the price for all of our sins by the shedding of his blood, which we as believers should not take lightly. Just because the price was paid does not mean that we should go around sinning. We have to try to be better Christians every day.

Mark 14:23-24 - Jesus' blood was shed not only for our sins, but also for us as a people. That shows his love for us, and we can never repay him. We should try to live our lives daily for the love of God.

Conclusion:

The blood of Jesus did a lot for the body of Christ. Some say the blood covers us, protects us, makes us whole and renews us. It does all of that, but the first thing it does is loves us. Everyone who chooses to live the Christian life are first loved by the blood.

NOTES:

_____

_____

_____

_____

_____

_____

_____

_____

_____

_____

_____

_____

_____

_____

_____

_____

_____

_____

_____

_____

_____

_____

_____

CHRIST:

The Lord has blessed us with His Word. All we have to do is be hearers, believers and doers of the Word.

Galatians 2:20 -I am crucified with Christ: nevertheless I live; yet not I, but Christ liveth in me: and the life which I now live in the flesh I live by the faith of the Son of God, who loved me, and gave himself for me.

Matthew 16:15-17 — He said unto them, But whom say ye that I am? And Simon Peter answered and said, Thou art the Christ, the Son of the living God. And Jesus answered and said unto him, Blessed art thou Simon Bar-jona: for flesh and blood hath not revealed it unto thee, but my Father which is in heaven.

1 John 2:22 - Who is a liar but he that denieth that Jesus is the Christ? He is antichrist, that denieth the Father and the Son.

Points to Consider:

Galatians 2:20 - Once the word shows us Christ, we see that I am Christ and Christ is me. That's the reason we live, because it's Christ that lives in us.

Matthew 16:15-17- Only God can reveal the truth about him and his Son. As believers we have to turn our ear to God. Only he can reveal that Jesus is his Son. He can reveal so much more to us if we just stop to learn.

1 John 2:22 - Every human that does not believe is not of Christ, they are the antichrist and they live in darkness.

Conclusion:

The word Christ is more than just the first word in Christmas, or just a great man that walked the earth. Only God can reveal the true Christ in our lives. Once we get the revelation, Christ dwells in us and we in him. This shows that there is no other way into the kingdom of God but by the name of Christ. There are no tricks that you can try, or anybody you can call, but the name Jesus Christ. If you've never heard of Jesus, you can know him for yourself. It's your choice. Ask God to reveal his Son Jesus , the Christ.

NOTES

_____

_____

_____

_____

_____

_____

_____

_____

_____

_____

_____

_____

_____

_____

_____

_____

_____

_____

_____

_____

_____

_____

CHURCH:

The Lord has blessed us with His Word. All we have to do is be hearers, believers and doers of the Word.

1 Timothy 3:5 - (For if a man know not how to rule his own house, how shall he take care of the church of God?)

Colossians 1:17-18- And he is before all things, and by him all things consist. And he is the head of the body, the church, who is the beginning, the firstborn from the dead; that in all things he might have the preeminence.

Ephesians 5:25 - Husbands, love your wives, even as Christ also loved the church, and gave himself for it.

Points to Consider:

1 Timothy 3:6 - If a man is in Christ he is the head of his house and he has to take his place in his own home before he can try to lead the church.

Colossians 1:17- Christ is before all things. By him all things consist. He is head of the church, but the church is the beginning of the first born when it comes to mankind on earth.

Ephesians 5:25 - We should love our wives as Christ loves the church. Christ is the husband of the church, and gave himself for it.

Conclusion:

These scriptures show the relationship between the church and the family. Men should love their wives as Christ loved the church. The church should be the beginning in our lives, the head, the start, our everything. As a household we should try to get our household in order, if not, it is impossible to run the place that we love so much, the church.

NOTES:

DEATH:

The Lord has blessed us with His Word. All we have to do is be hearers, believers and doers of the Word.

Psalm 23:3-4 - He restoreth my soul: he leadeth me in the paths of righteousness for his name's sake: Yea, though I walk through the valley of the shadow of death, I will fear no evil for thou art with me; thy rod and thy staff they comfort me.

John 5:24 — Verily, verily I say unto you, He that heareth my word, and believeth on him that sent me, hath everlasting life, and shall not come into condemnation; but is passed from death unto life.

John 8:50-51 — And I seek not mine own glory: there is one that seeketh and judgeth. Verily, verily I say unto you, If a man keep my saying, he shall never see death.

Points to Consider:

Psalm23:3-4 - God restores our soul and he also leads our path in life. Even though we have evil on every side, we should never fear death because the Lord is with us always. As believers this should comfort us.

John 5:24 — If we hear the word of God and believe in him and his word, even in death, condemnation or bad times, we shall have everlasting life.

John 8:50-51 - One of the benefits of being a believer is that we shall never die, but live on in heaven forever and ever.

Conclusion:

Death has been looked at in several ways. Some say it's a sad time because loved ones pass from earth to heaven or hell. Some say it's a great time because that person or loved one has moved from earth to heaven to be with God where they will never have to deal pain or suffering again. The Lord shows us that as believers when our time on earth is done, we don't die, we move into everlasting life in heaven, with God. There's no need to fear because believers live on through all eternity.

NOTES:

_____

_____

_____

_____

_____

_____

_____

_____

_____

_____

_____

_____

_____

_____

_____

_____

_____

_____

_____

FAITH:

The Lord has blessed us with His Word. All we have to do is be hearers, believers and doers of the Word.

Matthew 17:20 - And Jesus said unto them, Because of your unbelief: for verily I say unto you, If ye have faith as a grain of mustard seed, ye shall say unto this mountain, Remove hence to yonder place; and it shall remove; and nothing shall be impossible unto you.

Mark 11:20 — And in the morning, as they passed by, they saw the fig tree dried up from the roots.

Luke 7:50 — And he said to the woman, thy faith hath saved thee; go in peace.

Points to Consider:

Matthew 17:20 - If we have faith as small as a grain of mustard seed, we can speak and all of the mountains in our lives will be removed. There shall be nothing that is impossible in our lives.

Mark 11:20 — All we have to do is believe God for all things. First, speak it, and believe it in our heart, and it shall be done. For the fig tree to dry up, Jesus spoke to it and it was done. If we just believe in God, we can speak things onto our lives.

Luke 7:50 - Just a little faith can save us in whatever it is we're dealing with in life and we can live in peace.

Conclusion:

Faith is not about God, No, No, No! Faith is about us. If we just believe a little, as a mustard seed, that will make all the difference in our lives. If you're not a believer, pray for God's grace to help you build your faith. You need to hear the word and speak the word if you want the mountains to move in your life.

NOTES:

_____

_____

_____

_____

_____

_____

_____

_____

_____

_____

_____

_____

_____

_____

_____

_____

_____

_____

_____

_____

_____

FELLOWSHIP:

The Lord has blessed us with His Word. All we have to do is be hearers, believers and doers of the Word.

11 Corinthians 6:14 - Be ye not unequally yoked together with unbelievers: for what fellowship hath righteousness with unrighteousness? And what communion hath light with darkness?

1 John 1:6-7 - If we say we have fellowship with him, and walk in darkness, we lie, and do not the truth: But if we walk in the light, as he is in the light, we have fellowship one with another, and the blood of Jesus Christ his Son cleanseth us from all sin.

Ephesians 5:9-11 - (For the fruit of the Spirit is in all goodness and righteousness and truth;) Proving what is acceptable unto the Lord. And have no fellowship with the unfruitful works of darkness, but rather reprove them.

Points to Consider:

11 Corinthians 6:14 — As believers we should not fellowship or be unequally yoked together with unbelievers or unrighteousness. God says that light should not commune with darkness because they don't mix. They are like oil and water.

1 John 1:6-7 - Some may say that they are of God, but if they are walking in darkness. They are liars and the truth is not in them, (the people that play God). If we truly walk with God we are in the light and we fellowship one with another. The blood covers us and cleanses us from all of our sins.

Ephesians 6:14 - The fruit of God are great fruit and fruit of light. We should not fellowship with the fruit of unrighteousness because these are fruits of darkness and not of God.

Conclusion:

Fellowship is all about choices. The people that we fellowship with is our choice to make, but remember that God cannot and will not fellowship with darkness. He never has and he never will.

Notes:

_____

_____

_____

_____

_____

_____

_____

_____

_____

_____

_____

_____

_____

_____

_____

_____

_____

_____

_____

_____

_____

God:

The Lord has blessed us with His Word. All we have to do is be hearers, believers and doers of the Word.

Matthew 1:23 - Behold, a virgin shall be with child, and shall bring forth a son, and they shall call his name Emmanuel, which being interpreted is, God with us.

Mark 12:32 - And the scribe said unto him, Well, Master, thou hast said the truth: for there is one God, and there is none other but he.

John 4:24 - God is a Spirit: and they that worship him must worship him in spirit and in truth.

Philippians 4:19 - But my God shall supply all your need according to his riches in glory by Christ Jesus.

Points to Consider:

Matthew 1:23 — Mary would have a son and his name would be called Emmanuel, meaning God with us. He live in every Christian today. All we have to do is allow him to shine in us.

Mark 12:32 - There is only one God. Not your car, or your money, but one God. As a body of believers, let's stop looking other places for God. He's supposed to live in us!!

John4:24 - God is a Spirit, and as believer's we must worship him in spirit and in truth.

Philippians 4:19 - God will supply all our needs according to his time table. We must believe God, have faith and trust.

Conclusion:

People seem to have many different gods, for some it's money, jobs, Allah, or Buddha, but there is only one true God. God tells us that he is always with us, even when we don't want him. He's that kind of God. If we want God to rule our lives, we must believe him in spirit and in truth. Have faith and trust that he will supply all your needs.

NOTES:

_____

_____

_____

_____

_____

_____

_____

_____

_____

_____

_____

_____

_____

_____

_____

_____

_____

_____

_____

_____

_____

GLORY:

The Lord has blessed us with His Word. All we have to do is be hearers, believers and doers of the Word.

Psalm 84:11 - For the Lord God is a sun and a shield: the Lord will give grace and glory: no good thing will he withhold from them that walk uprightly.

Luke 2:14 - Glory to God in the highest, and on earth peace, good will toward men.

Philippians 4:19 - But my God shall supply all your need according to his riches in glory by Christ Jesus.

Romans 11:36 - for of him, and through him, are all things: to whom be glory for ever Amen.

Points to Consider:

Psalm84:11 - Great news!! The sun and shield are of God. He gives us his grace and glory and promises believers that no good thing will be withheld from them. That's what I call glory!!

Luke 2:14- The glory of God is for all believers. He wants us to have peace here on earth and good will and glory toward all men.

Philippians 4:19 - Another thing that falls under glory is that God will supply all our needs as believers in Christ Jesus.

Romans 11:36- All things are for God, through God, and to God. All things on earth are for God's glory.

Conclusion:

God's glory is everything that is good here on earth, the sun, shield, grace, heavenly peace, and the supplying of our needs. We should be thankful for the grace and glory of God everyday that we live.

NOTES:

_____

_____

_____

_____

_____

_____

_____

_____

_____

_____

_____

_____

_____

_____

_____

_____

_____

_____

_____

_____

GIFT:

The Lord has blessed us with His Word. All we have to do is be hearers, believers and doers of the Word.

Matthew 7:11 - If ye then, being evil, know how to give good gifts unto your children, how much more shall your Father which is in heaven give good things to them that ask him?

John 4:10 - Jesus answered and said unto her, If thou knowest the gift of God and who it is that saith to thee, Give me to drink; thou wouldest have asked of him, and he would have given thee living water.

Romans 6:23 - For the wages of sin is death; but the gift of God is eternal life through Jesus Christ our Lord.

11 Corinthians 9:15 - Thanks be unto God for his unspeakable gift.

Points to Consider

Matthew 7:11 - If the devil can give good gifts to his people, how much more can God do for the believers in Jesus Christ.

John 4:10 — If we knew the gifts of God, we as believers would not have to look somewhere else. We would see that all gifts that we need comes from him.

Romans 6:23 - God's greatest gift to all believers is eternal life through Jesus Christ.

11 Corinthians 9:15 - We should be very thankful because we know the truth.

Conclusion:

A gift is more than just something that you give on Christmas or birthdays. The gift of God is greater than the gifts of the devil. All we have to do is look up to God for the things we need. He has paid the price for the ultimate gift to the body of Christ. We should believe, trust God, give him the highest praise, and be thankful.

NOTES:

_____

_____

_____

_____

_____

_____

_____

_____

_____

_____

_____

_____

_____

_____

_____

_____

_____

_____

_____

_____

GRACE:

The Lord has blessed us with His Word. All we have to do is be hearers, believers and doers of the Word.

John 1:13-14- Which were born, not of blood, nor for the will of the flesh, nor of the will of man, but of God. And the word was made flesh, and dwelt among us, (and we beheld his glory as of the only begotten of the Father,) full of grace and truth.

Romans 3:23-24 - for all have sinned, and come short of the glory of God; Being justified freely by his grace through the redemption that is in Christ Jesus.

11 Corinthians 12:9 — And he said unto me, My grace is sufficient for thee: for my strength is made perfect in weakness.

Points to Consider

John 1:13 - Jesus was not born of the flesh, nor the will of man, but he was born of grace and truth.

Romans 3:23 - All have sinned and come short of the glory of God, but we as believers are set free by the grace of God.

11 Corinthians 12:9 — As we walk here on earth, experiencing ups and downs, happy and sad days, we can rest assured that his grace is sufficient. It makes us strong when we're weak.

Conclusion:

Grace is for God's people here on earth. It was through grace that the Lord sent Jesus to earth to deliver us from sin. His grace covers our weaknesses and helps us from day to day. Let's enjoy everyday of our lives, living in God's grace.

NOTES:

_____

_____

_____

_____

_____

_____

_____

_____

_____

_____

_____

_____

_____

_____

_____

_____

_____

_____

_____

_____

HOLY:

The Lord has blessed us with His Word. All we have to do is be hearers, believers and doers of the Word.

Exodus 20:8 - Remember the Sabbath day, to keep it holy.

Psalml45:17 - The Lord is righteous in all his ways, and holy in all his works.

Isaiah 6:3 - And one cried unto another and said, Holy, holy, holy, is the Lord of hosts: the whole earth is foil of his glory.

Revelation 22:11 — He that is unjust, let him be unjust still: and he that is righteous, let him be righteous still: and he that is holy, let him be holy still.

Points to Consider

Exodus 20:8 - Keep the Sabbath day holy. In everyday life we should give one day out of our busy week to God, and fellowship with our sisters and brothers in Christ.

Psalm 145:17 - The Lord is holy and righteous in all ways and works. There is no wrong in God or Christ.

Isaiah 6:3 — There is nothing on earth that is holier than our Lord and Savior Jesus Christ. We all are foil of his glory, and in part are holy also.

Revelation 22:11 - Unjust or still unjust, filthy or still filthy, all we can say is thank God the righteous is still righteous, and the holy is still holy.

Conclusion:

Holy is more than a word that we sing in a song, or just an empty phrase. The Sabbath is holy, and all the works and ways of God to the ends of the earth are holy, because they were made by him. The best thing however, is that we as believers are holy because we were made by God. We should look at ourselves as holy, holy, holy unto the Lord and Savior Jesus Christ.

NOTES:

_____

_____

_____

_____

_____

_____

_____

_____

_____

_____

_____

_____

_____

_____

_____

_____

_____

_____

_____

_____

LIGHT:

The Lord has blessed us with His Word. All we have to do is be hearers, believers and doers of the Word.

Psalm 27:1 — The Lord is my light and my salvation; whom shall I fear? The Lord is the strength of my life; whom shall I be afraid?

Psalm 119:105 - Thy word is a lamp unto my feet, and a light unto my path.

Matthew 5:16 - Let your light so shine before men, that they may see your good works, and glorify your Father which is in heaven.

1 John 1:7 -But if we walk in the light, as he is in the light, we have fellowship one with another, and the blood of Jesus Christ his Son cleanseth us from all sin.

Points to Consider:

Psalm 27:1 - The Lord is the light of my world, and my salvation. I shall fear nothing because he is my strength.

Psalm 119:105 - The word of God is our light and life. He will lead our path if we allow him to.

Matthew 5:16 - The light in us should shine everyday, and God should get all the glory.

1 John 1:7 — If we walk in the light of God, he will lead us and wash away our sins.

Conclusion:

God's light leads us out of darkness, is our salvation and strength, and washes away our sins. It provides guidance for our feet and our paths. Let's glorify God by allowing our lights to shine daily.

NOTES:

KINGDOM:

The Lord has blessed us with His Word. All we have to do is be hearers, believers and doers of the Word.

Colossians 1:12-13- Giving thanks unto the Father, which hath made us meet to be partakers of the inheritance of the saints in light: Who hath delivered us from the power of darkness, and translated us into the kingdom of his dear Son.

11 Timothy 4:18 - And the Lord shall deliver me from every evil work, and will preserve me unto his heavenly kingdom: to whom be glory for ever and ever: Amen.

James 2:5 - Hearken, my beloved brethren, Hath not God chosen the poor of this world rich in faith, and heirs of the kingdom which he hath promised to them that love him?

John 3:3 - Jesus answered and said unto him, Verily, verily, I say unto thee, except a man be born again, he cannot see the kingdom of God.

Romans 14:17 - For the kingdom of God is not meat and drink; but righteousness, peace, and joy in the Holy Ghost.

Matthew 6:33 - But seek ye first the kingdom of God, and his righteousness; and all these things shall be added unto you.

Points to Consider:

Colossians 1:12-13 — If we want to become partakers of the inheritance of the things of God, we have to become partakers of the kingdom of his dear Son, Jesus Christ.

11 Timothy 4:18 - The Lord has a select group in mind to inherit his kingdom. Those that are rich in faith shall inherit the kingdom of God.

James 2:5 - The Lord shall deliver us from evil and preserve for us a place in his heavenly kingdom where we'll live forever and ever!

John 3:3 - How do we enter into the kingdom? We must be born again, that is accepting Jesus as Lord and Savior.

Romans 14:17 - The kingdom of God is not the physical things of this life, but the kingdom of God is spiritual. Once we allow God to rule and reign in our lives the fruits of righteousness, joy, and peace will be exemplified.

Matthew 6:33 - God doesn't want us to be overly concerned about the things of this world. He wants us to concentrate on the things of God. If we do this we will find all the blessings in life that we need.

Conclusion:

God created the kingdom for every man on earth, but it's going to be up to you if you want to live in the kingdom. Some ask, what must I do to become a partaker of the kingdom? The scriptures clearly tells us that we must be born again. Become rich in faith and allow the Lord to deliver you from evil, then you too can become a member of the kingdom of God and enjoy all that he has for you.

NOTES:

_____

_____

_____

_____

_____

_____

_____

_____

_____

_____

_____

_____

_____

_____

_____

_____

_____

_____

_____

_____

_____

_____

LOVE:

The Lord has blessed us with His Word. All we have to do is be hearers, believers and doers of the Word.

John 13:34-35 — A new commandment I give unto you, That ye love one another; as I have loved you, that ye also love one another. By this shall all men know that ye are my disciples, if ye have love one to another.

John 15:12-13 — This is my commandment, that ye love one another, as I have loved you. Greater love hath no man than this, that a man lay down his life for his friends.

1 Timothy 6:10 - For the love of money is the root of all evil: which while some coveted after, they have erred from the faith, and pierced themselves through with many sorrows.

1 John 4:18-1 There is no fear in love; but perfect love casteth out fear: because fear hath torment. He that feareth is not made perfect in love.

Corinthians 13:13 - And now abideth faith, hope, charity(love), these three; but the greatest of these is charity(love).

Points to Consider:

John 13:34-35 - God commands us to love one another. Why? because of the love that he has for us. If he can love us with all of our faults and shortcomings then surely we should be able to love one another .When we walk in love others can see that we are a part of God's family. We're acting just like our Daddy.

John 15:12-13 - We should love each other the same way God loves us. He loved us so much that he gave his life for us. What great love the Father has for us.

1 Timothy 6:10 - There can be an evil side to love, and that is the love of money or anything that we put before God. Money itself is not evil, but when we allow it to have preeminence in our lives it becomes evil.

1 John 4:18 - There is no fear in love. If we let the love of God rule in our lives we will not be afraid of anything.

1 Corinthians 13:13 — Love supersedes all spiritual gifts. The word says that without love we're nothing.

Conclusion:

Love is a whole lot more than the words we speak. Love is an action. Because God loved, he gave and when we begin to truly love, we will give of ourselves just as Jesus did. Remember of all spiritual gifts, love is the greatest.

NOTES:

OBEY:

The Lord has blessed us with His Word. All we have to do is be hearers, believers and doers of the Word.

Acts 5:28-29 - Saying, Did not we straightly command you that ye should not teach in this name? and, behold, ye have filled Jerusalem with your doctrine, and intend to bring this man's blood upon us. Then Peter and the other apostles answered and said, We ought to obey God rather than men.

Colossians 3:22 — Servants, obey in all things your masters according to the flesh; not with eye service, as men pleasers; but in singleness of heart, fearing God:

Hebrews 13:17 - Obey them that have the rule over you, and submit yourselves: for they watch over your souls, as they must give account, that they may do it with joy, and not with grief: for that is unprofitable for you.

Ephesians 6:1 - Children obey your parents in the Lord: for this is right.

Points to Consider:

Acts 5:28-29 - As believers we must always be obedient.. It doesn't matter what man says or what we have to deal with, we should always obey God.

Colossians 3:22 - We should always obey our mater, which is Christ Jesus. As believers we shouldn't get angry or conform to our pleasures, but obey God.

Hebrews 13:17 - Children should submit to their parents because they watch over their souls. Parents are also accountable and must watch over their children with joy.

Ephesians 6:1 - Children should obey their parents for in so doing they are also obeying God.

Conclusion:

Obeying is not only a demand, it's a choice to do what's right.. The bible tells us that we must first obey God over man because he is the ruler of all. We shouldn't get angry but just be obedient to his word. Parents and children must be obedient for we're all accountable to God.

NOTES:

_____

_____

_____

_____

_____

_____

_____

_____

_____

_____

_____

_____

_____

_____

_____

_____

_____

_____

_____

_____

_____

_____

_____

Peace:

The Lord has blessed us with His Word. All we have to do is be hearers, believers and doers of the Word.

John 14:27 - Peace I leave with you, my peace I give unto you: not as the world giveth, give I unto you. Let not your heart be troubled, neither let it be afraid.

Ephesians 2:14 - For he is our peace, who hath made both one, and hath broken down the middle wall of partition between us.

Philippians 4:7 — And the peace of God, which passeth all understanding, shall keep your hearts and minds through Christ Jesus.

Colossians 3:15 —And let the peace of God rule in your hearts, to the which also ye are called in one body; and be ye thankful.

Points to Consider:

John 14:27 - God has left with us his God kind of peace, a peace that we cannot get from the world. Don't allow trouble to enter your heart or allow your heart to get full of fear.

Ephesians 2:14 - God did not just give us peace, but as believers he is our peace and has broken down all walls in our lives.

Philippians 4:7 - God's peace surpasses all understanding, so when you don't understand what's going on in your life the peace of God can still cover you as long as you keep your mind stayed on him.

Colossians 3:15 - Let peace rule in your life and in your heart. We are a part of the body of Christ and we should be thankful for the peace of God.

Conclusion:

The bible shows us that peace cannot be given from one man to another but true peace can only be given by God. The good thing about that is that no man can take it away from us. God's peace does not allow trouble or fear to penetrate your heart. It tears walls of trouble that we deal with on a daily basis. God's peace gives us understanding that we would never see without God. We should ask God to give us inner peace so that we can experience a little bit of heaven here on earth.

NOTES:

_____

_____

_____

_____

_____

_____

_____

_____

_____

_____

_____

_____

_____

_____

_____

_____

_____

_____

POWER:

The Lord has blessed us with His Word. All we have to do is be hearers, believers and doers of the Word.

Proverbs 18:21 — Death and life are in the power of the tongue: and they that have it shall eat the fruit thereof.

Matthew 28:17-18 - And when they saw him, they worshipped him: but some doubted. And Jesus came and spake unto them, saying, All power is given unto me in heaven and in earth.

John 1:11-12-He came unto his own, and his own received him not. But as many as received him, to them gave he power to become the sons of God, even to them that believe on his name.

11 Timothy 1:7- for God has not given us a spirit of fear: but of power, and of love, and of a sound mind.

Points to Consider:

Proverbsl8:21 - Life and death lies in our tongue. We can kill people with our tongue, so we need to choose our words carefully. We also have the power to breed life into our lives.

Matthew 28:17-18 - The Lord has all power over heaven and earth, and we should worship him because of it.

John 1:11- Some may receive you as a believer, and some may not, but to those that receive you or God, the Lord will give power to become the sons of God.

1 Timothy 1:17- God did not give us the spirit of fear, but he gives us power to move mountains in our lives, and the spirit to love one another.

Conclusion;

Power is more than just something that precedes the word horse, and placed within cars, or something used when we work out. Power comes from God, and believers have the power of life and death in their tongue. All who receive God will be given this power. God also gives us love and soundness of mind. God has all power over heaven and earth, and we too should have power over all things in our lives.

NOTES:

_____

_____

_____

_____

_____

_____

_____

_____

_____

_____

_____

_____

_____

_____

_____

_____

_____

_____

_____

_____

_____

_____

PRAYER:

The Lord has blessed us with His Word. All we have to do is be hearers, believers and doers of the Word.

Matthew 21:22 - And all things, whatsoever ye shall ask in prayer, believing, ye shall receive.

James 5:15-16 - And the prayer of faith shall save the sick, and the Lord shall raise him up, and if he have committed sins, they shall be forgiven him. Confess your faults one to another, that ye nay be healed. The effectual fervent prayer of the righteous man availeth much.

Matthew 21:13- And said unto them, It is written, My house shall be called a house of prayer; but ye have made it a den of thieves.

Acts 6:4 - But ye will give yourselves continually to prayer, and to the ministry of the word.

Points to Consider:

Matthew 21:22 - We should know that whatever we ask for in prayer, if we believe, the Lord will give it to us. Prayer is our gateway to heaven.

John 5:15-16- The prayer of faith shall save the sick and the Lord shall raise them up and forgive their sins, but that's not all, if we confess one to another and pray for each other we will be healed. The fervent, sincere prayer of the righteous makes tremendous power available.

Matthew 21:13 - The church is a place of prayer, and not a place for evil deeds. We should always see the Lord's house as a holy place

Acts 6:4 - We should be in constant communication with God. Prayer is our way of talking to our Father. We should always look for opportunities to minister the word of God wherever we go.

Conclusion;

Prayer is more than something we do at night before going to bed, or just something we do in the morning when we awaken. Prayer is the way we talk to God, and because of that we receive power. We receive power to heal the sick, to be forgiven of our sins, and to know that whatever we ask for, as long as we believe, the Lord will grant it to us. The church is a place of prayer. We should be in prayer in season and out of season, in good times and in bad times. The effects of prayer coming from the righteous makes tremendous power available.

NOTES:

REDEEMED:

The Lord has blessed us with His Word. All we have to do is be hearers, believers and doers of the Word.

Psalm 103:4 - Who redeemeth thy life from destruction; who crowneth thee with loving kindness and tender mercies.

Psalm 107:2 - Let the redeemed of the Lord say so, whom he hath redeemed from the hands of the enemy.

Isaiah 51:11 — Therefore the redeemed of the Lord shall return, and come with singing unto Zion; and everlasting joy shall be upon their head; they shall obtain gladness and joy; and sorrow and mourning shall flee away.

Galatians 4:5 - To redeem them that were under the law, that we might receive the adoption of sons.

Points to Consider:

Psalm 103:1 — The Lord has redeemed us from destruction and from the evils of the devil. Believers will be crowned with his love, kindness, and tender mercies.

Psalm 107:2 — God has redeemed us and we should gladly say so. We've been redeemed from the hands of the enemy.

Isaiah 51:11- When God comes back for his people , the redeemed shall sing songs unto Zion, and everlasting joy shall fall on the people of Jesus Christ. They shall live a life free of sorrow.

Galatians 4:5 - Believers are redeemed from the law and adopted as children of God.

Conclusion;

To be redeemed is to be set free from destruction and from the hands of the enemy. We are delivered and given the crown of love and kindness. God will put a new song in our mouth and crown us with everlasting joy and freedom from sorrow. We are adopted as his children, so we should let others see the glory of God in us.

NOTES:

_____

_____

_____

_____

_____

_____

_____

_____

_____

_____

_____

_____

_____

_____

_____

_____

_____

_____

_____

_____

_____

_____

RIGHTEOUSNESS:

The Lord has blessed us with His Word. All we have to do is be hearers, believers and doers of the Word.

Psalm 111 :2-3 -The works of the Lord are great, sought out of all them that have pleasure therein. His work is honorable and glorious: And his righteousness endureth forever.

Matthew 5:6 - Blessed are they which do hunger and thirst after righteousness: for they shall be filled.

Romans 10:10-11 - For with the heat man believeth unto righteousness; and with the mouth confession is made unto salvation. For the scripture saith, Whosoever believeth on him shall not be ashamed.

11 Corinthians 5:21 — For he hath made him to be sin for us, who knew no sin; that we might be made the righteousness of God in him.

Points to Consider:

Psalms 111 :2-3 - Whosoever does the work of the Lord or the work that he has called us to do is honorable, glorious and righteous. His righteousness last forever.

Matthew 5:6 — If we hunger and thirst after righteousness we shall be blessed and obtain mercy.

Romans 10:10-11 - Our hearts should be filled with righteousness and our mouth must confess our salvation. We should never be ashamed of our beliefs or righteousness.

11 Corinthians 5:21 - God made Jesus to be sin for us so that we might be made righteous.

Conclusion:

We have been made right with God because of what Jesus did. Being righteous is about doing the work that you were put on this earth to do. We should hunger and thirst after righteousness. Never be ashamed of your beliefs, for God's righteousness is honorable and glorious and by it we obtain mercy. God gave his Son for our sins so that we could have this righteousness.

NOTES:

_____

_____

_____

_____

_____

_____

_____

_____

_____

_____

_____

_____

_____

_____

_____

_____

_____

_____

_____

_____

_____

_____

_____

SAVE:

The Lord has blessed us with His Word. All we have to do is be hearers, believers, and doers of the Word.

Matthew 1:21 - And she shall bring forth a son, and thou shalt call his name Jesus: for he shall save his people from their sins.

Matthew 18:11-12 - For the son of man is come to save that which was lost. How think ye? If a man have an hundred sheep, and one of them be gone astray, doth he not leave the ninety and nine, and goeth into the mountains, and seeketh that which is gone astray?

Acts 4:12 - Neither is there salvation in any other: for there is none other name under heaven given among men, whereby we must be saved.

Points to Consider:

Matthew 1:21 - This verse tells of the coming of a Savior who would save the people from their sins. The only way we can be saved is through his name because he paid the price for our salvation.

Matthew 18:11-12 - We see here that Jesus (the son of man) came to save everyone. He loves us so much that if one of us would astray, he would leave all the others to search for the one that's lost. God's love for us is so powerful that he won't allow us to stay lost.

Acts 4:12-There is no other name whereby man can be saved except the name of Jesus because he gave his life for us and made it possible that all we have to do is believe or-, his name and we cars be saved and receive everlasting life.

Conclusion:

Mary will bring forth a son and shall call his name Jesus. He shall save his people from their sins. What wonderful news, that Jesus would deny himself of his heavenly pleasures to come down into a mean and hateful world just so that you and I could be saved. Glory to the Lamb of God for such a wonderful and unselfish, act. Hallelujah!!!

NOTES:

_____

_____

_____

_____

_____

_____

_____

_____

_____

_____

_____

_____

_____

_____

_____

_____

_____

_____

_____

_____

_____

_____

Sin: Part 1:

The Lord has blessed us with His Word. All we have to do is be hearers, believers and doers of the Word.

Psalm 38:18 - For I will declare mine iniquity; I will be sorry for my sin.

John 8:7 - So when they continued asking him, he lifted up himself and said unto them, he that is without sin among you, let him first cast a stone at her.

Romans 6:23 - For the wages of sin is death; but the gift of God is eternal life through Jesus Christ our Lord.

11 Corinthians 5:21 - For he hath made him to be sin for us, that knew no sin, that we might be made the righteousness of god in him.

Points to Consider:

Psalms 38:18 - We should see our sin and have a repentant heart.

John 8:7 - All have sinned, therefore we cannot sit in judgment on others.

Romans 6:23 - Because we have all sinned, we shall die. Thanks be to God that through Jesus Christ our Lord we can have eternal life.

11 Corinthians 5:21 - Jesus took our place as sinners so that we could take his place as the righteous.

Conclusion;

All men are sinners and at some point in our lives the Holy Spirit helps us to see our sinful condition. It is at this point that we should repent and turn away from our sins. The payoff for sin is death and for that reason every man will die, but because we give our lives over to Christ and repent of our sins we can have eternal life. God loves us so much that he allowed Jesus to bare all our sins so that we can live victoriously.

NOTES:

_____

_____

_____

_____

_____

_____

_____

_____

_____

_____

_____

_____

_____

_____

_____

_____

_____

_____

_____

_____

_____

_____

SIN: PART 11:

The Lord has blessed us with His Word. All we have to do is be hearers, believers and doers of the Word.

11 Samuel 12:13 - And David said unto Nathan, I have sinned against the Lord, and Nathan said unto David, The Lord also hath put away thy sin; thou shalt not die.

Romans 3:23-24 - For all have sinned, and come short of the glory of God; Being justified freely by his grace through the redemption that is in Christ Jesus.

1 John 3:8-9 - He that committed sin is of the devil; for the devil sinneth from the beginning. For this purpose the Son of God was manifested, that he might destroy the works of the devil.

Points to Consider:

11 Samuel 12:13 - David sinned against God, but because he had a repentant heart, God forgave him. Nathan said you shall not die, meaning that eternal life was still available to David.

Romans 3:23-24 - Even though we've all sinned, if we believe in Christ, our faith in him puts us in a position of justification just as if we'd never sinned).

1 John 3: 8-9 — Sin is the work of the devil, and for that reason Jesus came into the world to destroy the devil's work.

Conclusion;

We make choices everyday of our lives. We make a choice of doing good or evil. Remember that sin is of the devil, but Jesus came to deliver us from sin. With God's help we can overcome sin. Jesus came so that we would have the power to overcome sin, Hallelujah!! Thank you Jesus for dieing for my sins.

NOTES:

_____

_____

_____

_____

_____

_____

_____

_____

_____

_____

_____

_____

_____

_____

_____

_____

_____

_____

_____

_____

_____

_____

Spirit:

The Lord has blessed us with His Word. All we have to do is be hearers, believers and doers of the Word.

Psalm 51:10-11 — Create in me a clean heart, and renew a right spirit within me. Cast me not away from thy presence; and take not thy holy spirit from me.

Isaiah 61:1- The Spirit of the Lord is upon me; because he hath anointed me to preach good tidings unto the meek; he hath sent me to bind up the broken hearted, to proclaim liberty to the captives, and the opening of the prison to them that are bound.

John 4:24 - God is a Spirit; and they that worship him must worship him in spirit and in truth.

11 Corinthians 3:17 - Now the Lord is that Spirit; and where the Spirit of the Lord is, there is liberty.

Points to Consider:

Psalms 51:10-11 — God can create in us a clean spirit and give us a clean mind therefore we should never turn away from his sweet holy spirit.

Isaiah 61:1- When the spirit of the Lord is upon us we are anointed to preach his word, bind the broken hearted, bring liberty to the captives, and open the prison doors to those that are locked up.

John 4:24 - God is a spirit, and those that worship him must worship him in spirit and in truth.

11 Corinthians 3:12- When we connect with God (the true Spirit), then and only then will we have found true freedom.

Conclusion;

There are many spirits in the world today, but there's only one Holy Spirit It is God's Spirit that cleans us up, anoints us to preach his word and live the life that he created us to live. We must worship God in spirit and truth because God is truth and he is a spirit.

NOTES:

_____

_____

_____

_____

_____

_____

_____

_____

_____

_____

_____

_____

_____

_____

_____

_____

_____

_____

_____

_____

_____

Teach:

The Lord has blessed us with his Word. All we have to do is be hearers, believers and doers of the Word.

Luke 4:31-32 - And came down to Capernaum, a city of Galilee, and taught them on the Sabbath days.

And they were astonished at his doctrine: for his word was with power.

Psalm 25:4-5 -Show me thy ways, O Lord; teach me thy paths.

Lead me in thy truth, and teach me: for thou art the God of my salvation: on thee do I wait all the day.

Matthew 22:32-33 -I am the God of Abraham, and the God of Isaac, and the God of Jacob? God is not the God of the dead , but of the living.

And when the multitude heard this, they were astonished at his doctrine.

Points to Consider:

Luke 4: 31-32 - Jesus was going into Galilee. The people were astonished or amazed because the Lord spoke with such authority. Even to the point that demons came out of a man at his word. This shows us what can happen when we allow the spirit of God to use us to teach the word with great authority. When the word of God is spoken with authority mighty things will be accomplished.

Psalm 25: 4-5 - David is sure in what he's asking God. He realizes that God's way is best, so he asks God to teach him your ways and lead me down the path that you have chosen for me. We too must be willing to allow the Holy Spirit to lead, guide and direct our paths. David also knew that God was his savior. Finally, David knew that he had to wait for God's appointed time, therefore he said that I will wait on the Lord.

Matthew 22: 32-33 - As Jesus teaches in Matthews, again the people are astonished at the authority with which he teaches. Jesus challenges the people to come up higher in their thinking. As we study and experience the word of God our thinking should change as the old passes away and the new begins to develop. My prayer is that God would teach me something new on a daily basis.

Conclusion:

David was sure in asking God to teach him his ways. Jesus taught with such authority that every unclean spirit had to obey. Jesus teaches a fresh, life changing word that astounded the multitudes. We see what can happen when the word goes forth in power. God has given us power today to teach with authority, but first we must ask God to teach us is ways. He will then empower us to help set the captives free and we will also have a life changing, refreshing word for his people. A word that will fill them with joy and hope. I challenge you to allow God to teach you his ways.

NOTES:

_____

_____

_____

_____

_____

_____

_____

_____

_____

_____

_____

_____

_____

_____

_____

_____

_____

_____

_____

_____

_____

WISDOM:

The Lord has blessed us with his Word. All we have to do is be hearers, believers and doers of the Word.

Proverbs 9:10-The fear of the Lord is the beginning of wisdom: and the knowledge of the Holy is understanding.

Ecclesiastes 7:12 - For wisdom is a defense: and money is a defense: but the excellency of knowledge is, that wisdom giveth life to them that have it.

Luke 2: 52 - And Jesus increased in wisdom and stature, and in favor with God and man.

Colossians 2: 3In whom are hid all the treasures of wisdom and knowledge.

Points to Consider:

Proverbs 9:10 - In order to receive wisdom we must first have the fear of the Lord (a reverential respect for God). The fear of the Lord helps to put boundaries in our lives. Those things that you would ordinarily do now you would reconsider because of the fear of the Lord developed in you.

Ecclesiastes 7:12 —Wisdom and money are a defense, but unlike money, wisdom offers life or light to a dead situation. Wisdom offers the ability to change a lives.

Luke 2:52 -Just as Jesus did, when we increase in wisdom and knowledge, we too will increase in favor with God and man. Favor is an asset as we proceed to fulfill the plan of God for our lives. It should be the desire of every believer to have the favor of God on their lives.

Colossians 2:3- All wisdom and knowledge is in the Father. We must seek his face in order to receive this wisdom and knowledge. As we study the word of God and seek his face in prayer we will increase in wisdom and knowledge.

Conclusion:

We evaluate success in life in many ways, sometimes according to our jobs, houses, cars, money, etc. God is the only one that can give us the wisdom we need to achieve true success in life. We should seek him for wisdom and knowledge to navigate in this life. It is only with the knowledge that we receive from God that we will reach our ultimate potential in this life. Praise God that as we seek him, he also blesses us with favor.

NOTES:

_____

_____

_____

_____

_____

_____

_____

_____

_____

_____

_____

_____

_____

_____

_____

_____

_____

_____

_____

_____

_____

_____

THE WORD:

The Lord has blessed us with His word. All we have to do is be hearers, believers, and doers of the word.

John 1:1 - In the beginning was the Word, and the Word was with God, and the Word was God

1 Peter 1:23 — Being born again, not of corruptible seed, but by the word of God, which liveth and abideth forever.

11 Timothy 4:2 - Preach the word; be instant in season, out of season; reprove, rebuke, exhort with all longsuffering and doctrine.

1 John 2:5 - But whoso keepeth his word, in him verily is the love of God perfected: hereby know we that we are in him.

Points to Consider:

John 1:1- The Lord is showing us how important the word is in our life. God is the Word.

1 Peter 1:23 — the only way we can be born again is first in the word of God. The word cannot be corrupted.

11 Timothy 4:2 - Preach the word in season, and out of season, in good and bad times. We should tell people about God. Now we are the word of God. Once we see that God is the word, we learn how to keep the word.

a. If we love God, He is going to share his word with us.

b. If we keep the word in our hearts, it becomes a part of us, and in return we become the word.

c. At this point the Lord gives us the power to preach his word to his people so the word can become word in their lives.

1 John 2:5 - We should keep His word. Where and how? By keeping the word in our heart. Once the word is in our heart no one can take it from us.

Conclusion:

In the beginning God was the Word and the Word was God, but now I am the word because the word is inside of me.

NOTES:

_____

_____

_____

_____

_____

_____

_____

_____

_____

_____

_____

_____

_____

_____

_____

_____

_____

_____

_____

_____

_____